SLANG

A POCKET GUIDE TO RAP WORDS & PHRASES

So you don't look stupid when trying to understand Hip Hop culture

PREFACE

Hip Hop originated in the Bronx borough of New York in the 1970s. For those over a certain age, hearing hip hop slang can sound like a foreign language. A unique vocabulary has been developed which can be utterly mystifying to outsiders. This mini illustrated 'dictionary' of hip hop words and sayings is here to rescue

FO SHIZZLE!

45

A pistol that takes a .45 caliber cartridge.

212

Private conversation with someone.

718

Area code in certain places in New York such as Brooklyn, Queens and The Bronx.

730

Angry or crazy. A code sometimes used by the law to refer to someone out of control or a danger.

808

Refers to a code for disturbing the peace.

Aiight

Alright. A greeting.

BALLER

A person who lives a rich and extravagant lifestyle. Flashy with the wealth.

BATTLE

A rap battle, a contest between rappers.

BEEF

To have a grudge, problem, feud or argument with someone.

BIRD

A kg of controlled substance packed in a brick.

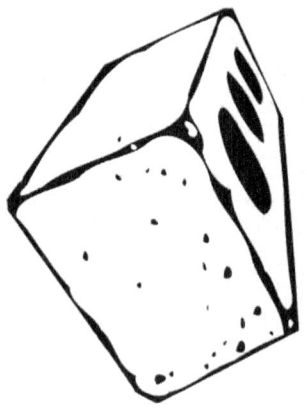

BITE

To steal another rapper's lyrics.

Girlfriend, darling or significant other.

BOOTY

Backside.

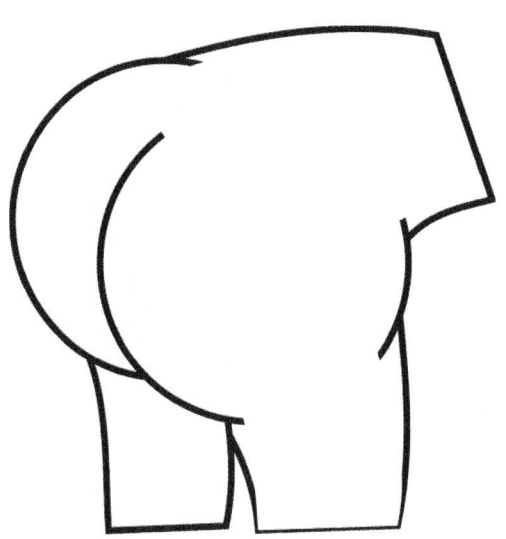

BOUNCE

To leave or depart a place or situation.

CAP

Bullet.

CHEDDER

Money.

CHEESE

Money.

CHILL

Relax.

CLOWNING

Making fun of someone or acting silly, messing around and having fun.

CRIB

House.

CRUNK

Crazy drunk or very excited.

DA BOMB

The bomb. Simply the best.

DAWG

A close and trusted friend.

Disc Jockey.

DIME

A very attractive girl. A perfect 10.

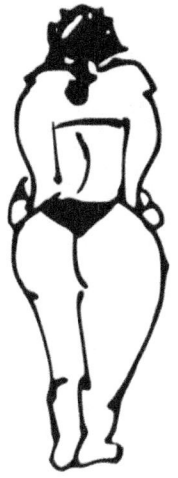

DIP

To leave. Let's go.

DISS

Disrespect.

DOPE

Something that is cool or appealing.

DOUGH

Money.

DUBS

Twenty inch rims.

FAM

Short for family, a close relationship between people you associate with. Expression of friendship.

FLOSSING

Showing off with designer clothes and expensive jewellery.

FLY

Cool.

FO SHIZZLE

For sure.

FREESTYLE

Improvise a rap.

FRESH

Cool, new.

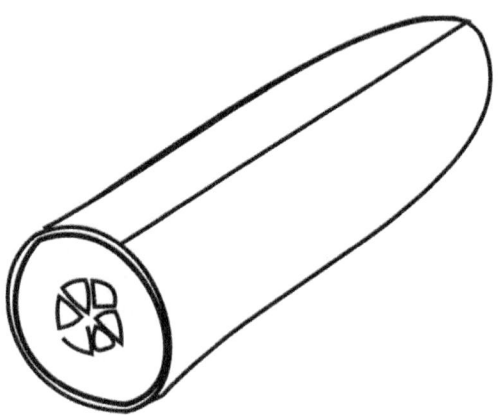

FRONT

Pretend to be someone you are not, especially pretending to be tough.

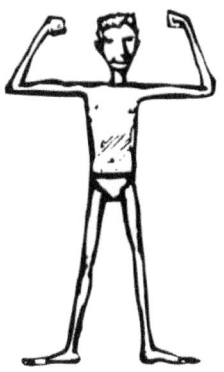

GHETTO BIRD

Police helicopter.

GOAT

Greatest of all time.

GOLD DIGGER

Someone who likes a person because of the amount of money they have.

GRILL

The mouth.

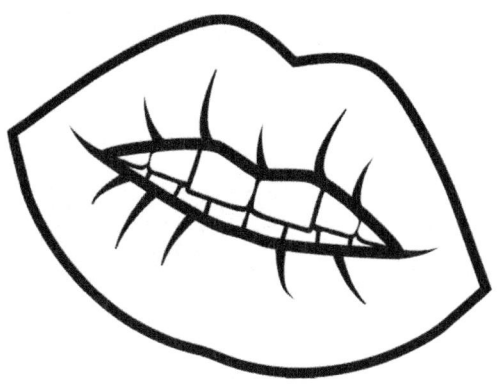

Working hard to make money.

HERB

Any drug but more commonly used for marijuana.

HIP HOP

Genre of music encompassing rapping, DJing and dancing.

HOE

A term used usually to describe a female.

HOMIE

A trusted and loyal friend.

HOOD

Your neighbourhood.

HUSTLE

Working smart to make money.

ICE

Diamonds.

MILKSHAKE

The female body and its movements.

MY BAD

My mistake.

#

Original gangster. Someone old school with extensive knowledge and experience. An expression of deep respect.

OLD SCHOOL

Retro.

ONES & TWOS

A DJ's turntable.

PEACE OUT

Goodbye.

PHAT

Cool.

PO PO

Police.

PUNK

An as*hole, coward or wimp.

RAP

Speak lyrics rhythmically.

RIDE

A car.

RIZZLE

Real.

SHAWTY

Usually used by men to describe an attractive female.

SHIZZLE

Sh*t.

SNITCH

Someone who passes on private information about a person. Often used when reporting criminal activity.

SPIT

Rap.

SQUAD

Your closest and most trustworthy group of friends. Your gang, posse, crew.

STUNTING

Someone showing off or putting on an act to get attention.

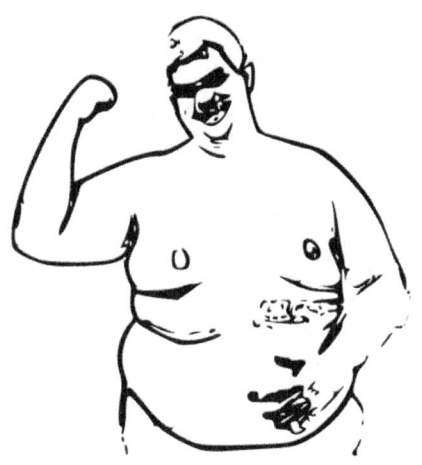

SWAG

Cool, stylish and confident manner.

TIGHT

Close friends with someone.

TRAP

A sub-genre of hip hop.

TRAP HOUSE

A house used to sell drugs.

TREE

Weed, pot.

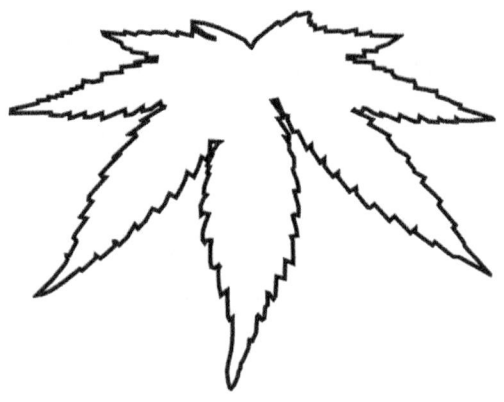

TRIPPING

High on drugs. Crazy.

WHACK

Not cool.

A nice car.

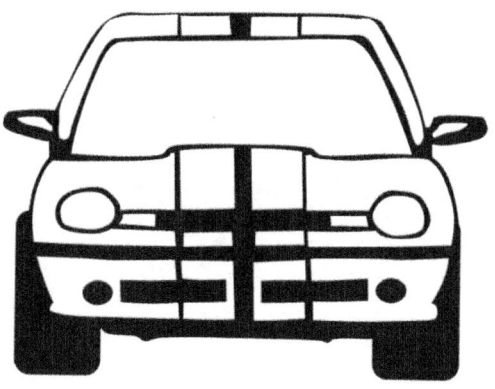

WORD

True, well said.

Y

Hey.

PEACE OUT
PEACE OUT
PEACE OUT
PEACE OUT
PEACE OUT
PEACE OUT
PEACE OUT
PEACE OUT
PEACE OUT
PEACE OUT
PEACE OUT
PEACE OUT

Printed in Dunstable, United Kingdom